MY CATECHISM

First steps in
Christian Faith

Graham Jeffery

First published 1990 in Great Britain by
KEVIN MAYHEW LTD
Rattlesden
Bury St Edmunds, Suffolk IP30 0SZ

ISBN 0 86209 121 7

Typesetting by Typestylers, Ipswich, Suffolk
Page make-up by Emma Bailey
Printed and bound in Great Britain by
The Five Castles Press Limited, Ipswich, Suffolk

MY CATECHISM

This life belongs to:

_____

And to God, too.
We mustn't
forget that

This Catechism contains
the shadows of one man's life . . .

and some other things to help me.

O Lord,
when you give
your servants grace
to begin any great matter,
help us to know
it is not the starting
of it only,
but the continuing
of the same
till it be thoroughly finished,
that yields the true glory,
through Jesus Christ
our Saviour.

It is finished

Amen

I was born in Bethlehem.
I lived most of my life in Nazareth.
I died outside the city walls of Jerusalem.
I live in the hearts of those who love me . . .
    and receive me.
(Matthew's Gospel, chapter 4, verses 18-22)

CONTENTS

*(Some things to know and believe
to my soul's health)*

	page
WHAT IS MY NAME?	11
Who gave me this name?	14
What did my godparents promise for me?	16
THE ARTICLES OF MY FAITH	17
The Apostles' Creed	18
The Lord's Prayer	32
The Ten Commandments	45
SEVEN SACRAMENTS FOR ONE CHURCH	65
The Two Great Sacraments	67
Holy Baptism	68
The Holy Communion	72
Five More Sacraments	74
Holy Matrimony	75
Ordination	77
Confirmation	82
Confession	88
Holy Unction	90
SOME WORDS TO COMFORT ME	91
St Patrick's Breastplate	92
Help me to be myself, Lord	93

WHAT IS MY NAME?

I'm not my clothes,
not my accent,
not my body,
not my arms and legs,
not my personality, even —
that can change in time.

I am myself,
and God loves me.

Who am I?
That's what I ask myself.
The thing that makes me
'me', and no one else in
the history of the world.

1.

I mean . . . what is my
name? What is the deep
meaning of myself?

2.

After all, I know where I
am. I look in the atlas for
that.

3.

And I know when I am.
I look at my watch (very
digital) for that.

4.

But who I am deep
down, God alone knows;
and one or two friends
who really believe in my
possibilities.

5.

Ah well. That's how it is
in life.
My friends call me all the
names in the world.

6.

But God just calls me.

WHO GAVE ME THIS NAME?

My godparents at my baptism,
in which I became a child of God,
a member of his family the Church,
and an inheritor of the
Kingdom of Heaven.

I am a child.

I am a brother.

God helps me
to become both.

I am baptized
in the name of the Father,
and of the Son,
and of the Holy Spirit.

WHAT DID MY GODPARENTS PROMISE FOR ME?

That I should renounce
the devil and all his works.

That I should believe
in God.

That I should
follow him.

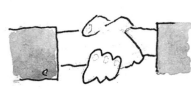

THE ARTICLES OF MY FAITH

THE APOSTLES' CREED

The illustration shows a boat bearing the words "Jesus of Nazareth preached here".

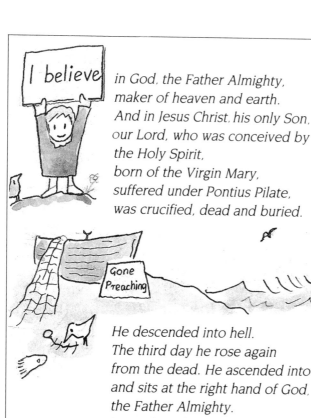

I believe in God, the Father Almighty,
maker of heaven and earth.
And in Jesus Christ, his only Son,
our Lord, who was conceived by
the Holy Spirit,
born of the Virgin Mary,
suffered under Pontius Pilate,
was crucified, dead and buried.

He descended into hell.
The third day he rose again
from the dead. He ascended into heaven,
and sits at the right hand of God,
the Father Almighty.
From there he shall come again,
to judge the living and the dead.
I believe in the Holy Spirit,
the holy catholic Church,
the communion of saints,
the forgiveness of sins,
the resurrection of the body,
and the life eternal.

I believe in God the Father almighty, maker of heaven and earth.

He made things visible . . .

He made things invisible . . .

God is the maker of all things,
the source of all life.
He makes the water fall
and the river flow.

He helps the little bird to fly.

He did not make the world
and leave it to run on its own.
He loves it, and all his children,
continuously.

Of course, there is much evil
in the world, too.
God is creating the world out of nothing.
He is creating love out of hatred,
light out of darkness.

We can do
everything
with Him

He needs our help
to do it.
God can do nothing
without us.
He can do everything
with us.
We can do nothing
without him.

And in Jesus Christ his only Son, our Lord.

Jesus is God's only Son.
I too am his son or daughter.
Jesus lived so that I might feel that.
Jesus lives, not to be different from me,
but to help me believe
I am God's own child too.

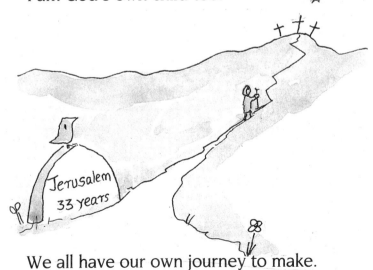

We all have our own journey to make.

Who was conceived by the Holy Spirit.
Born of the virgin Mary. . .

The whole of Jesus' life is God's idea.
God's conception of how a human life
could be. Relying only on love.
Loving his friends and family,
praying for those who rejected
and killed him.
And loving his friends to the very end.
Whatever else he did or did not do,
Jesus was successful in that.

But Jesus was Mary's idea, too.
She was the first person to believe in love,
and believe in Jesus. She believed in him,
and gave birth to him.
But don't forget Joseph, will you.
He wore his knuckles out,
knocking on all the doors in Bethlehem.
He was the man who found Jesus a stable
to be born in.
And built him a house to live in.
Joseph was the first to say:
'behold, I stand at the door
and knock.'

Can I come in please?

He descended into Hades.

. . . the place of departed spirits.
For God's love is for Abraham and Isaac,
who lived 2,000 years before Jesus,
as much for us,
who live 2,000 years (nearly)
after the crucifixion.
In this sense,
the first disciple to know
how much Jesus really loved him was . . .
Judas Iscariot.

The third day he rose again from the dead.

He ascended into heaven
and sits at the right hand of God,
the Father almighty.

From there he shall come again,
to judge the living and the dead.

JESUS of Nazareth died on a Friday afternoon, probably about three o'clock, and was buried quickly by two friends, before the sun went down. Saturday was the Sabbath, on which Jesus' friends rested, and remembered God their creator and saviour.

On Sunday, the first day of a new week, Jesus came to life in the hearts and lives of those who loved him. Those who loved him most, saw him most. Those who missed him most, saw him first — and realized his death was not a defeat at all, but a victory of love. The only victory worth having.

Even so, Jesus' friends believed together. By being together, they helped each other to believe. Thomas, for instance, who stayed away on his own, took longer to realize that Jesus was alive. Then he said the first Christian creed, 'My Lord and my God.'

After some time (the children of Israel called any longish time 'forty days') Jesus' friends knew for sure he was alive. At breakfast, at night-time, in the evening, in the garden, indoors . . . Jesus was alive with them in all these places. Only then were the disciples ready to 'settle down' . . . and live by faith and confidence at last, knowing Jesus was in heaven to meet them, too. Till then, God's Spirit would be enough, and more than enough.

For God's Spirit, which they experienced so strongly at Pentecost, was Jesus living inside them: instead of beside them. Only at Pentecost could they say, 'now not I, but Christ lives inside me.' Only at Pentecost was Jesus' work completed. Or, you may say, it began again for the second time.

I believe in the holy ghost,

I shall renew the face of the earth

the holy catholic Church,

I'm never alone

the communion of saints,

even when I die

especially then

THE LORD'S PRAYER

It wasn't just the words he said.
It was the way he lived his life.

OUR FATHER WHO ART IN HEAVEN
  Hallowed be thy name.
  Thy kingdom come.
  Thy will be done
  on earth as it is in heaven.

  Give us today
    the things we need,
  Forgive us our trespasses,
    as we forgive those
    who hurt us.

  Lead us not into temptation
    but deliver us from evil.

What I ask in it.

A place for myself in God's world,
that I may bless others,
and not hurt them.
I ask a place for them, too.
And for all people.
One person's place in the world
does not exclude anyone else,
or push them out.

I ask for the things I need:
  food, a home, a family,
  work to do, friendship.

I ask forgiveness of my sins,
  which God gives freely, day by day.
  I need never be unsure of that.

I ask for God's kingdom to come,
  for his name or meaning
  to be kept safe, and observed.

I ask for God's glory.

They are all my brothers and sisters

Our Father . . .

God is the Father or Mother
of all his children.
He loves me and calls me
his 'special' child.
He loves me as if I were his only friend.

Even so, it's nice to say 'Our Father'
when we talk to him. It's a quick way
of remembering the whole human race.

bless this World

Well done

. . . who art in heaven

Heaven is 'where God is'.
Where there is peace and fairness,
and love and kindness and truth,
that place *is* heaven.
Of course,
we will not reach 'heaven' properly
till we die,
and see God's love for us clearly.
But even here on earth,
there is 'heaven' to be made,
and work to be done.

Hallowed be thy name.

May God's meaning be kept holy.
Not just his church cleaned,
or the brass polished.
But the thing that makes goodness good . . .
may we keep this sacred,
and hold on to it.

Thy kingdom come.

God's kingdom is not the same
as Israel or Canaan.
It is not the same as any country today,
though some countries
may be much closer to it than others.
God's kingdom is where people love,
honour and respect each other.
That country, or village,
or home, or person,
is part of God's kingdom.

Jesus of
Nazareth
Lives here

Thy will be done . . .

Jesus didn't have to leave us a will,
written instructions in a solicitor's office,
safely kept. But he left us his example —
and more than that, God's Spirit.
May this 'will' be done here,
as it was in his first 33 years.
. . . on earth
as it is in heaven.

Give us today . . .

The things we need: food, friendship, family,
work to do. A chance to leave this world
as we would like to have found it.
Life comes to us breath by breath, though.
We have to do our best each day;
accept our failures,
know that God loves us. Then start again.
Tomorrow is another day.

Forgive us our trespasses . . .

The only certain thing in life is . . .
we will fail.
We will do the things we shouldn't.
Or not do the things we should.
There is no avoiding that.
The girl or boy who never made mistakes,
never made anything.
We should not be surprised
when we do wrong, then.
Just pray to God to avoid it.
Encourage ourselves with good friends
and activities,
and give ourselves a chance to grow.
Pray for our priests,
and other people, too.
The Church is a family of sinners.

even the little sparrow
needs
forgiveness

As we forgive those who trespass against us.

Pray for other people to be good.
They need our prayers.
Perhaps we will stop a world war
by praying for, and loving one person.
Think of that.
Remember too, how we need the prayers
and support of others.
No one can be good on their own,
without encouragement.
(Or if they can,
it is very heroic and unusual.)
Above all pray:

Lord, forgive me.
Lord, help me to forgive others.
Help me to know
that I am loved;
I am forgiven.

(4) Its no use Fido. You just don't understand. Can't you notice anything?

lick lick

(5) MY GAME WAS AN ABSOLUTE DISASTER

It didn't seem a disaster to me. It seemed rather a triumph

(6) Prepare to Smash

For instance. I liked the way you biffed the ball into the bushes. I liked it when you ran about and got puffed. I liked it when you patted me.

(7) But then. We dogs notice different things

Grr Grrr

SMASH

42

Lead us not into temptation.
Life is difficult enough,
without asking for trouble.
Though we will follow Jesus
'beyond the map',
to adventures or loneliness
we might prefer to have missed,
we must 'play it safe', too.
Be bold — but be careful.
Try to avoid 'holes in the road' —
places or circumstances
where we are likely to fall.

But deliver us from evil.
Though God follows us
into every failure,
or sin or evil place,
we must still try
to avoid them.
Say every day,
'deliver us
from evil' . . .
and believe that
in the end
he will.

For the kingdom, the power, and the glory are yours now and for ever. Amen.

THE TEN COMMANDMENTS

Ten for living
Two for loving

What are the Commandments God
has given me?

They are those which God gave to Moses
on Mount Sinai, written down
in Exodus, chapter 20.

The ten commandments were written
by Moses on two tablets of stone.

They were carried all the way
from Mount Sinai to Canaan.

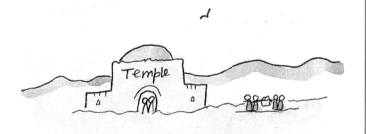

They were put in the Temple
King Solomon built for them.
But the best home for them
is our hearts.

Because if people love each other and help each other

And love God first, We mustn't forget that

④

And don't steal each other's lives or wives

Or reputations or golf clubs

⑤

Then we'll be in Canaan though we're only fifteen miles from Egypt

And sand gets in our eyes

⑥

49

50

My duty to God:

A bird's first duty is to understand the sky

The first four Commandments say:

1 You shall have no other gods but me.
2 You shall not make any graven image.
   Nothing can take my place.
3 You shall not use my name lightly.
   My meaning for you in the world.
4 You shall keep my day holy.
   Six days you shall work
   and do all you have to do.
   But one day a week belongs to me.

all days belong to Him, really

My duty to God:

1 You shall have no other gods but me.
   Nothing shall take my place. No job.
   No cars. Nothing I have made or done.
   (They are all God's gifts to us,
   and we must worship him alone.)

no one can
describe the sky

2 You shall make to yourself
   no graven image.
   Nothing shall take my place.

My duty to God:

3 You shall keep my name holy.
    My meaning for you in the world.
    Do not use my name lightly.
    Remember I love you so much,
    you can never describe me:
    never draw pictures of me.
    Whatever words you use
    to describe me,
    or my love for you,
    I am always beyond them.

My duty to God:

4 You shall keep my day holy.
    Six days shall you work,
    and do all you have to do.
    But one day every week
    belongs to me.

I dive and I soar
and I fly
every day

Sun Monday Tues Wednesday
Thurs Fr

and one day a week
I look at the sky

My duty to my neighbour:

There are
other birds
in the sky

The next six Commandments say:

5 You shall honour your father and mother.
6 You shall not kill.
7 You shall not take your neighbour's wife,
    break up his home, his family,
    the nearest thing he has.
    No one is so hurt
    as through their wife,
    husband or children.
8 You shall not steal
    or take away
    your neighbour's property.
9 You shall not steal his good name,
    or reputation.
    That belongs to him as well.
    You shall not tell lies about him
    or bear him false witness.

My duty to my neighbour:

10 You shall not covet his wife,
        family, job, reputation, car,
        position in the world.
        For if you want something too much,
        you may be led to steal it,
        to kill your neighbour for it,
        to speak unkindly, unfairly of him;
        to steal his wife or family from him,
        and his position in the world.

My duty to my neighbour:

5 You shall honour your father and mother.
　　Your first two neighbours —
　　when they look after you,
　　and feed you, and love you,
　　and let you go . . .
　　When they are old,
　　pray for them especially.

my parents
taught me
to fly

My duty to my neighbour:

6 You shall not kill.
   Your neighbour needs space
   to live his own life.
   His life is not only his body,
   and being able to breathe and eat.
   It is his wife (or husband),
   his family, his home,
   his interests and his
   position in the world.
   Do not kill your neighbour
   in any way.
   By word, cruelty, or neglect.
   Your first duty is to help others
   towards life — not take it away.

My duty to my neighbour:

In more detail

7 You shall not commit adult-ery —
　　or take away the nearest adult friend
　　your neighbour has —
　　wife . . . or husband.
　　Encourage your neighbour
　　when he does good things.
　　Ask God to bless his wife and family.
　　God blesses people first,
　　　then homes,
　　　　then villages,
　　　　　then towns and countries.

Don't
　push me
　　out of
　　　my nest

Help God
to bless
the world
by blessing
our families
and homes.

My duty to my neighbour:

There's enough sky for everyone

8 You shall not steal —
    or take away
    your neighbour's life, wife,
    family, reputation,
    or anything he has.

not even his tea-spoons

My duty to my neighbour:

9 You shall not bear false witness . . .
    tell lies about your neighbour.
    You shall not kill your neighbour
    in your speech.

My duty to my neighbour:

10 You shall not covet or want too much . . .
   your neighbour's car, wife,
   husband, job, house or gifts.
   However much he's got,
   he's not you.

63

What I learn by them:

To love God with all my heart
and soul and strength,
and to love my neighbour
as myself.

SEVEN SACRAMENTS
FOR ONE CHURCH

I'm still around, child.
Look and you will find me.
In church and sacrament I come alive;
in preaching of my word,
but in your life most clearly.

Here, I want to settle down
and find that home denied to me
at Bethlehem.

Your life is all the space I need
to bless you first
and afterwards the world.

Somebody's been here before

he's still here

THE TWO GREAT SACRAMENTS

or, How to get to heaven
on bread and wine,
and a little water

Holy Baptism — in which I belong.
Holy Communion — in which I am fed.

The Five Lesser Sacraments

Holy Matrimony — in which I have a family.
Holy Confession — in which I am forgiven.
Confirmation — in which I am blessed
and make my own promises.
Ordination — in which I am called to serve.
Holy Unction — in which I am blessed again.

HOLY BAPTISM

One more river to cross

In baptism I am immersed in your life, Lord.
With all my difficulties,
and all my disabilities.
I belong to you,
and am a member of your family.
You belong to me,
and will never let me go.

How long does it take
to be christened, child?
Not just twenty minutes
on a Sunday afternoon.
With the rector saying God loves you
like a father, like a brother,
like the heart-beat inside you.

But to be really christened,
really put into Christ,
takes so many years, *Who will*
so much failure, *I send?*
so much starting again.

I think to be christened, Lord,
takes all my life long,
and all your love
to accomplish it.

*I'll have
a go, Lord*

This font is a most revolutionary piece of architecture.

1.

I pour water from it once, and it says God is our Father.
And not just our Father, but the Father of everyone in the world.

2.

I pour it again to show God is our brother (or sister).
But as God is more than mother or father or brother or sister . . .

3.

I pour it again to say he is the Spirit inside us that binds us to each other.
And makes us brothers and sisters and children and friends.

4.

5.

Long live the revolution!

THE HOLY COMMUNION

A meal in which everyone can share.

At Holy Communion we recall the life
and death of Jesus of Nazareth.
How he lived on earth, loved us,
died while still loving us,
when it seemed all hope was gone.
Then on the third day
he rose again in our hearts,
and lives for ever.

In Holy Communion,
we set forth his life.
   We proclaim it,
     we share in it,
       we receive it.
Then we go out into the world
in the power of God's Spirit.

Dear Lord,
we thank you
for all your goodness
and loving kindness
to us and to all people.
We bless you for our creation,
preservation, and all the blessings
of this life.
But, above all,
for your inestimable love
in the redemption of the world,
through our Lord Jesus Christ,
for the means of grace
and for the hope of glory.

FIVE MORE SACRAMENTS

or Signs of God's presence.

A prayer for my home: Holy Matrimony
A prayer for my church: Ordination
A prayer for myself: Confirmation
A prayer of sorrow: Confession
A prayer when I am sick: The Laying on of Hands

HOLY MATRIMONY

In which man and woman become
'one flesh' and 'family'
by making their promises
to each other.

I Joseph take you Mary to my
wedded wife   for better or worse
for richer   or poorer
in sickness   or in health
A MEN

Not everyone gets married.
Some people marry
and their marriages 'break down'.

May God bless my mother and father,
and all who have no family.
Amen.

Dear Lord and Father,
you shared at Nazareth
the life of an earthly home.
Bless our homes also,
we ask you.
Live in them,
bless our mothers and fathers
and all who love us.
Help them to love and follow you.
May we respect them
and honour you in all things.
Keep our families safe.
Keep our world safe.
Amen.

ORDINATION

Bishop
Shepherd of the flock

**Priest or
Minister**
Servant of the people

**Deacon or
Deaconess**
(means servant, too)

The bishop, priest and deacon
are three 'orders'
or ways of serving God's family.
There are other ways . . .
and some Christians
have no ordained ministers at all.

May God bless all those
who are set apart,
and offer themselves for this work.
May God bless my work, too.
It is just as valuable.
I am set apart and chosen, too.

Dear Lord,
You alone work great marvels.
Bless that gift of yours to me,
your Church.
Bless our bishops, priests and deacons,
and all the congregations
they look after.
Bless your ancient people, the Jews,
and keep them safe.
Bless all those who love you.
You know who they are,
please make them strong.
And may I follow you,
and love you for ever.
Amen.

THE BISHOP

The bishop is the shepherd of the flock. He carries a shepherd's crook to remind himself that 'the Lord is our shepherd', and God knows each of us by name, and leads us and feeds us.

Jesus, the good shepherd, laid down his life for us. And still lays down his life for us daily, through those who love us.

Dear Lord,
Please bless the bishop
who confirms me.
May he love me,
and teach me,
and call me by name.
May he feed the people
with your words,
and follow you himself.
Then it will be safe
to follow him.

THE PRIEST OR MINISTER

The priest or minister is the servant of his people. When he is 'ordained' it is a step down, not a 'step up'.

Armies have generals. Navies have admirals. But the Church only has servants. Even so, they do lead their people by preaching God's love. And they celebrate the 'Mass' or 'Supper of the Lord', and feed all God's children there.

The priest or minister declares God's forgiveness to us.

Dear Lord,
Please bless our priests and ministers,
and those who serve us,
and tell us about you.
They need your help, too.
Perhaps I might become one,
and even if I do not,
I am still your obedient servant.
Amen.

THE DEACON

The deacon helps the priest at Holy Communion. He holds the chalice, and reads the gospel.

Most deacons go on to become priests and look after a parish.

We've come to see how you are

Dear Lord,
Please bless our deacons.
May they serve you faithfully,
and love and serve us also.
For Jesus' sake.

CONFIRMATION

In Confirmation, the bishop blesses me, and asks the gift of God's Spirit for me, all my life long.

Who will I send, and who will go for me?

Here I am send me

A Prayer for My Confirmation

Defend me, O Lord,
with your heavenly grace,
that I may continue your child for ever,
and daily increase in your Holy Spirit
more and more,
until I come to your kingdom.

What to take with me.

Love suffers long, and is kind.
Love is not easily provoked.
Love bears all things,
believes all things,
hopes all things,
Love makes everything possible.
(from 1 Corinthians 13)

Paul's description of what my life can be.

JESUS was twelve years old when he realized that Joseph the carpenter was not his only father, but that he had a Father in heaven who loved him, looked after him and would never let him go.

This was a very painful moment for Mary and Joseph. They felt they were losing him. But really, they were helping Jesus to grow up. And stand, with God's help, on his own two feet.

You may not be twelve years old exactly at your Confirmation — you may be a hundred! But your Confirmation, and the bishop's blessing of you, is the time you call God your Father or Mother. And begin to realize your Mummy and Daddy — your parents on earth — are not the only ones who love you. Though they are, after God, the first. So please pray for them especially on your Confirmation day.

The only story we have of Jesus' childhood is in Luke's Gospel, chapter 2, verse 41.

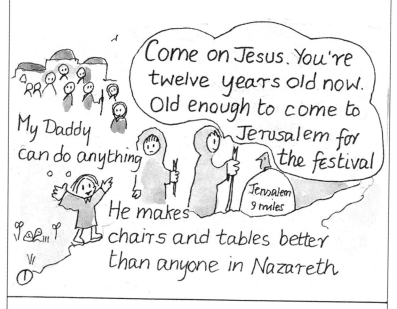

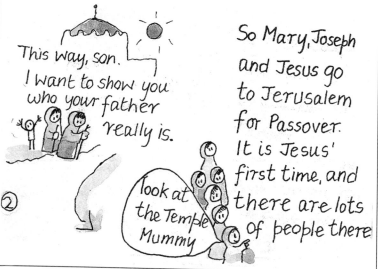

CONFESSION

For when I fall over, which I will do constantly.

In Confession I say sorry to God for the times I hurt him, or do bad things deliberately.

All Christians sin or do wrong. All people do wrong . . . but Jesus' followers are perhaps more conscious of it.

God loves me, whether I sin by thought or word or deed. He always forgives me, the moment I turn to him, or think of turning to him.

The priest or minister declares this forgiveness to me, before every Communion and at most services. It is sometimes called the 'Absolution'.

Your priest or minister is a sinner, too. Please pray for him or her, and speak to them if you ever need comfort or encouragement. Anything you say to them is in confidence, heard by them, but really only for God's ears. Only God loves you utterly, completely. Your priest or minister only tries to.

Dear Lord,
Forgive me when I do wrong;
or forget you,
or fail to do the good I can.
All my life long
I will make mistakes —
that is to be expected.
But help me to remember
you are always there
to welcome me back,
to help me start again,
to comfort me.
And so, Lord,
knowing you always forgive me,
I follow you,
as well as I can.

HOLY UNCTION

The laying on of hands when I am sick.
Sometimes my head is anointed with oil.

Lord, you are still here,
please bless me when I am sick,
and make my life
a blessing to others.

SOME WORDS
TO COMFORT ME

ST PATRICK'S BREAST-PLATE

Christ be with me, Christ within me,
Christ behind me, Christ before me,
Christ beside me, Christ to own me,
Christ to comfort and restore me.
Christ beneath me, Christ above me,
Christ in quiet, Christ in danger.
Christ in hearts of all who love me,
Christ in mouth of friend and stranger.

I have
my shell

hedgehogs only
have prickles

Help me to be myself, Lord.
I must never be afraid to be that.
There is, after all,
only one 'me' in the world.
Only one person
with my particular gifts or weaknesses.

Therefore Lord,
however badly I feel,
however far I fall,
I always know you are there
to welcome me back,
because you made me;
you've got no one else like me
for the job or life
you have in mind.

I am me

Lo, I am with you always.

I was glad when they said to me,
we will go into the house
of the Lord.

*Even so, Lord Jesus,
come, quickly.*